HELP WITH HOMEWORK

MATHS ESSENTIALS

9+

Key Stage 2

Maths Essentials

Key skills for key stages
Links school and home working

Autumn Publishing

number values

Write these numbers in words.

For example:
321,857 = three hundred and twenty-one thousand, eight hundred and fifty-seven

a. 53 fifty-3 three

b. 653 six hundred, and fifty-three

c. 1653 One thousand, six hundred and fifty-three

d. 21,653 twenty-one thousand, six hundred and fifty-three

e. 721,653 Seven hundred and twenty-one thousand, six hundred and fifty-three.

Write these numbers in numerals.

a. Two thousand, three hundred and four 2,304

b. Nine thousand, one hundred and eighty 9,180

c. Eleven thousand, three hundred and seventy-six 11,376

d. Fifty thousand, six hundred and four 50,604

e. Two hundred and one thousand, eight hundred and ninety 201,890

Order these numbers from the smallest to the biggest.

a. 7436, 5345, 4201, 6032 4201, 5345, 6032, 7436

b. 5642, 5386, 5740, 5900 5386, 5642, 5740, 5900

c. 6945, 6201, 6001, 6389 6001, 6201, 6389, 6945

get it?

To order the digits, start from the left each time.

When you order decimal numbers, it can help if you line them up underneath each other.

For example:

0.60
0.06

0.60 is bigger than 0.06

get it?

0.06 is "nought point nought six".

0.60 is "nought point six nought".

Order these decimals from the smallest to the biggest.

a. 0.01, 0.90, 0.59, 0.73 0.01, 0.59, 0.73, 0.90

b. 0.10, 0.05, 0.21, 0.09 0.05, 0.09, 0.10, 0.21

negative numbers

Complete this number line with negative numbers.

-10 -9 -8 -7 -6 -5 -4 -4 -3 -1 0 1 2 3 4 5 6 7 8 9 10

Order these numbers as they would appear on the number line.

a. 9, 10, -1, -7, -3, -10 -10, -7, -3, -1, 9, 10

b. 7, -7, 4, -2, -1, 9 -7, -2, -1, 4, 7, 9

c. 5, 0, -1, 1, -8, -4 -8, -4, -1, 0, 1, 5

stick a reward sticker here!

addition and subtraction

Add the units first, then add the tens, then the hundreds and finally the thousands.

Remember to carry digits over to the correct columns.

For example:

	Th	H	T	U
	1	4	5	5
+		2	3	5
	1	6	9	0
			1	

5 + 5 = 10 so carry the ten into the tens column.

Add these numbers.

a

	H	T	U
	5	7	3
+	3	3	5
	9	0	8

b

	H	T	U
	6	7	5
+	2	1	5
	8	9	0

c

	Th	H	T	U
	1	2	4	3
+	1	8	0	7
	3	0	5	0

d

	Th	H	T	U
	2	4	7	2
+	1	1	5	5
	3	6	2	7

e

	Th	H	T	U
	6	0	3	4
+	1	2	6	5
	7	2	9	9

f

	Th	H	T	U
	5	1	4	2
+	1	3	6	8
	6	5	1	0

Subtract the units first, then subtract the tens, hundreds and finally the thousands.

If you don't have enough units, exchange (or borrow) a ten for 10 units. If you don't have enough tens, exchange a hundred for 10 tens. If you don't have enough hundreds, exchange a thousand for 10 hundreds.

For example:

	Th	H	T	U
	0	15	12	1
	~~1~~	~~6~~	~~3~~	2
–		7	4	5
		8	8	7

Subtract these numbers.

a

	H	T	U
	6	4	3
–	3	5	4

b

	H	T	U
	6	7	2
–	2	2	4

c

	Th	H	T	U
	1	2	9	0
–		7	2	7

d

	Th	H	T	U
	2	2	8	9
–	1	1	9	5

e

	Th	H	T	U
	3	7	7	7
–	1	2	7	5

f

	Th	H	T	U
	4	0	2	4
–	1	1	9	5

get it?

Start from the right each time. You can exchange or borrow from the columns to the left.

1 ten = 10 units

1 hundred = 10 tens

1 thousand = 10 hundreds

stick a reward sticker here!

shapes

stick a reward sticker here!

Learn the names of these 2-dimensional (2-D) shapes.

Can you draw lines of symmetry on each shape to create mirror images? Which shape doesn't have a line of symmetry?

Parallelogram – opposite sides are equal and parallel

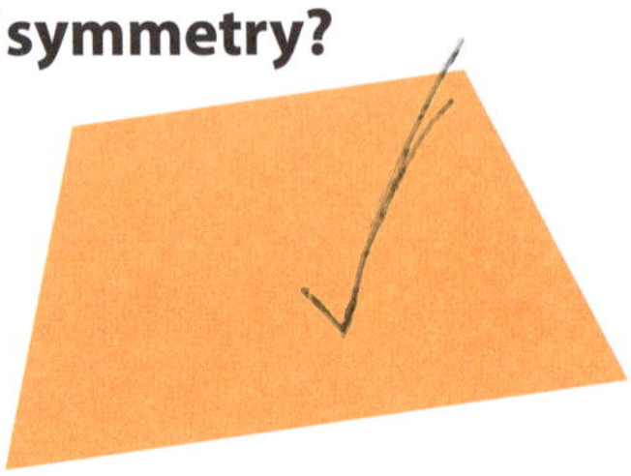

Trapezium – 2 sides are parallel

Square – 4 sides are equal, 4 right angles

Rectangle – opposite sides are equal, 4 right angles

Regular pentagon – 5 equal sides, 5 equal angles

Regular hexagon – 6 equal sides, 6 equal angles

Rhombus – 4 equal sides, opposite sides are parallel

Kite – adjacent sides are equal, no sides are parallel

Answer: True (T) or False (F) below.

1. A square has 4 equal sides and 4 right angles. [T]
2. A rectangle has equal opposite sides. [T]
3. A square is a quadrilateral. [T]
4. A trapezium has 1 line of symmetry. [T]
5. A rectangle has 4 lines of symmetry. [F]

Learn the names of these 3-dimensional (3-D) shapes.

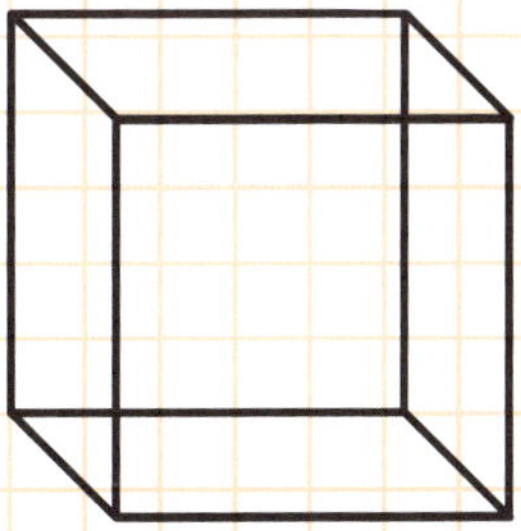

Cube

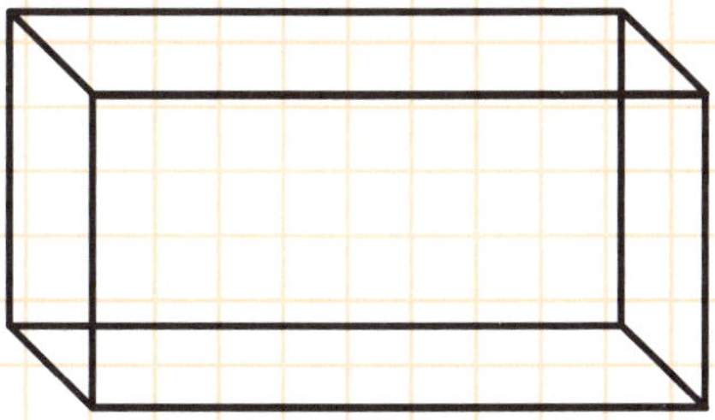

Cuboid

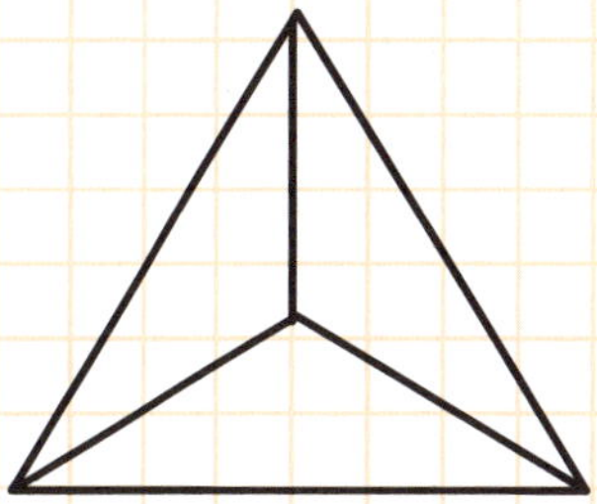

Triangular-based pyramid

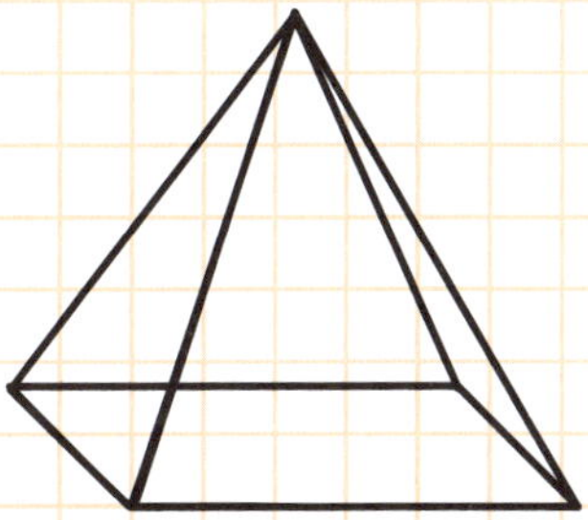

Square-based pyramid

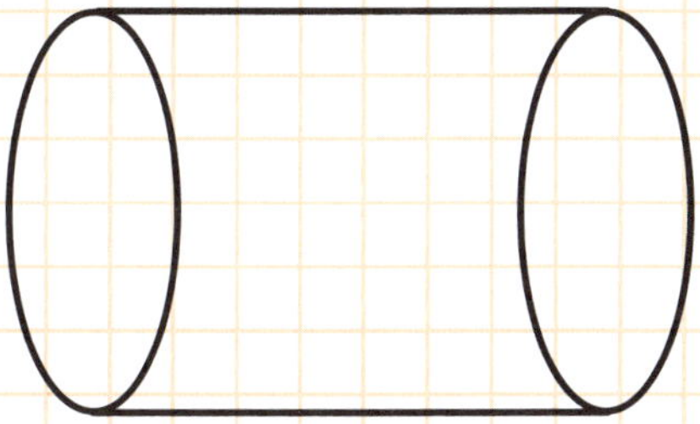

Cylinder

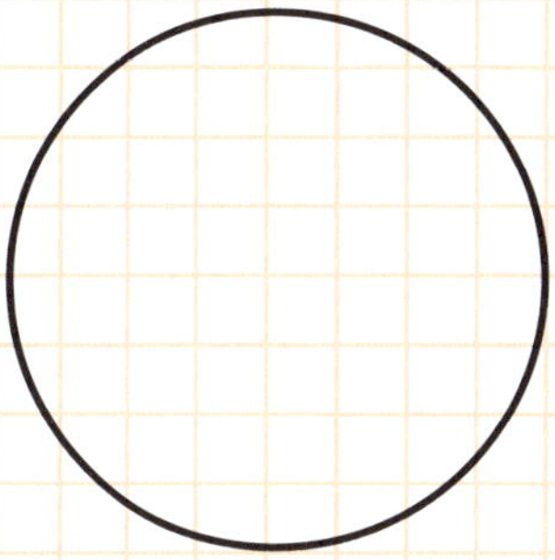

Sphere

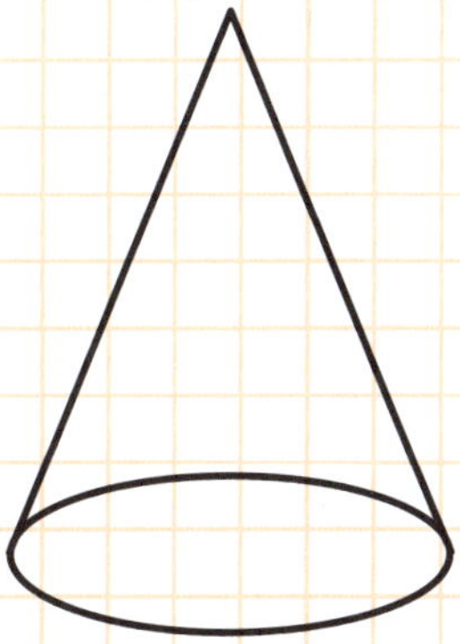

Cone

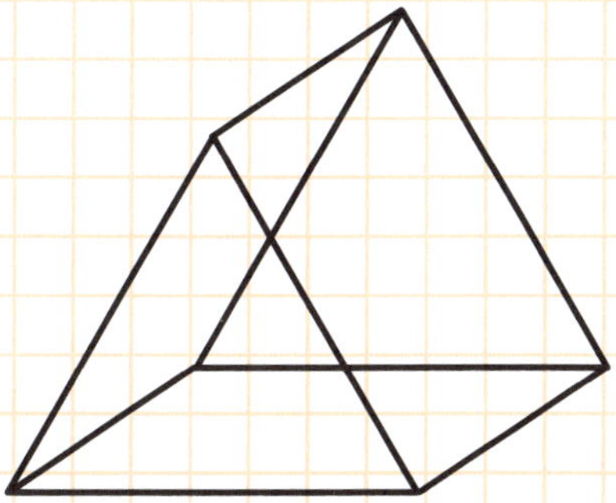

Triangular prism

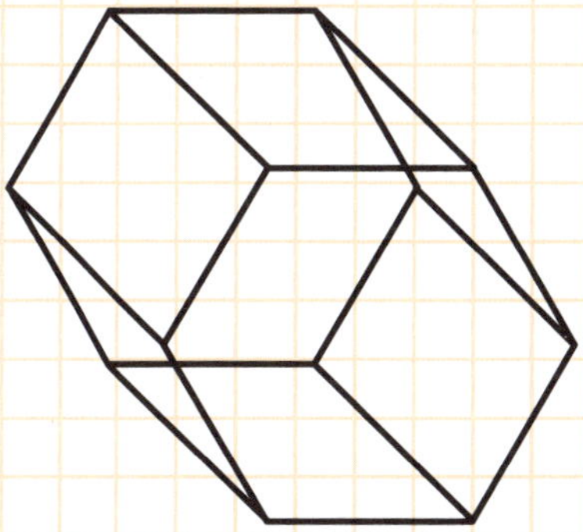

Hexagonal prism

Complete the table below:

Shape	Number of faces	Number of edges	Number of corners *(vertices)*
Cube	6	8	8
Square-based pyramid	5	9	5
Triangular prism	5	9	6
Cylinder	2	2	0

multiples and factors

stick a reward sticker here!

A **multiple** is the number you get when you multiply one number with another number, for example the multiples of 5 are 5, 10, 15, 20, 25, etc.

Count in 3s:

3	6	9	12	15	18	21	24	27	30

Count in 4s:

4	8	12	16	20	24	28	32	36	40

Count in 6s:

6	12	18	24	30	36	42	48	54	60

Count in 8s:

8	16	24	32	40	48	56	64	72	80

Circle the numbers that are multiples of 3. Which two numbers are also multiples of 6?

32 36 40 9 30 27 21

Circle the numbers that are multiples of 4. Which three numbers are also multiples of 8?

24 40 80 28 46 15 36

A **factor** is a number that will divide evenly (without a remainder) into another number, for example 3 is a factor of 6, 9 and 12, etc.

Find all the factors of 36:

1 x 36

2 x 18

3 x ___

4 x ___

6 x ___

Find all the factors of 24:

1 x 24

2 x ___

3 x ___

4 x ___

A **prime number** is only divisible by 1 and itself, for example 3 is a prime number.

Which of these are prime numbers? Circle them.

11 15 5 13 7 10 9 12

Work out what the missing numbers are.

For example:

6

3 **2**

49

7 ___

28

4 ___

30

15 ___

35

5 ___

get it?

even x even = even

odd x odd = odd

odd x even = even

division and multiplication

stick a reward sticker here!

Complete the multiplication grid.

The first answer is done to get you started.

X	7	5	6	2
3	21			
6				
8				
4				

get it?

When we multiply the numbers get bigger; when we divide the numbers get smaller.

Multiplication and division are **opposites**.

For example:
8 x 5 = 40, so 40 ÷ 8 = 5 and 40 ÷ 5 = 8

Write two divisions to match each multiplication.

5 x 6 = 30

30 ÷ 6 = 5

30 ÷ ___ = ___

5 x 11 = 55

55 ÷ ___ = ___

55 ÷ ___ = ___

7 x 4 = 28

28 ÷ ___ = ___

28 ÷ ___ = ___

8 x 6 = 48

48 ÷ ___ = ___

48 ÷ ___ = ___

Division is like **repeated subtraction**.

For example:

55 ÷ 11 = 5 is the same as: 55 – 11 – 11 – 11 – 11 – 11

Work out these divisions.

30 ÷ 5 = ____

30 –

70 ÷ 10 = ____

70 –

56 ÷ 7 = ____

56 –

You can work out divisions using repeated subtraction on a number line.

For example:

12 ÷ 3 = 4

12 11 10 9 8 7 6 5 4 3 2 1 0

Try it for yourself.

15 ÷ 3 = ____

15 14 13 12 11 10 9 8 7 6 5 4 3 2 1 0

20 ÷ 5 = ____

20 19 18 17 16 15 14 13 12 11 10 9 8 7 6 5 4 3 2 1 0

perimeter and area

stick a reward sticker here!

The **perimeter** is the distance around the edges of a shape.

Measure these shapes to find the perimeter.

a Perimeter = _____ cm

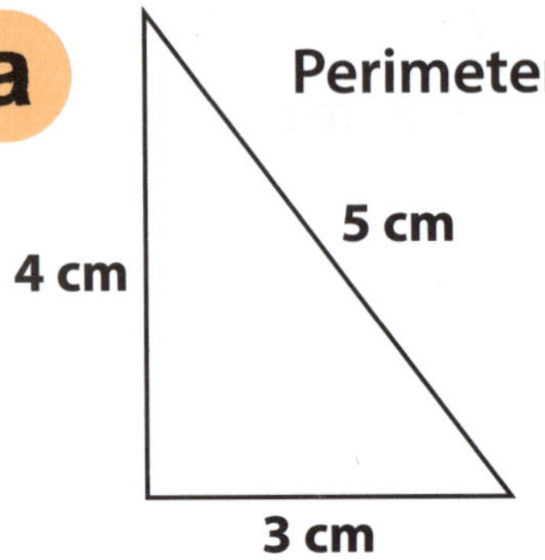

b

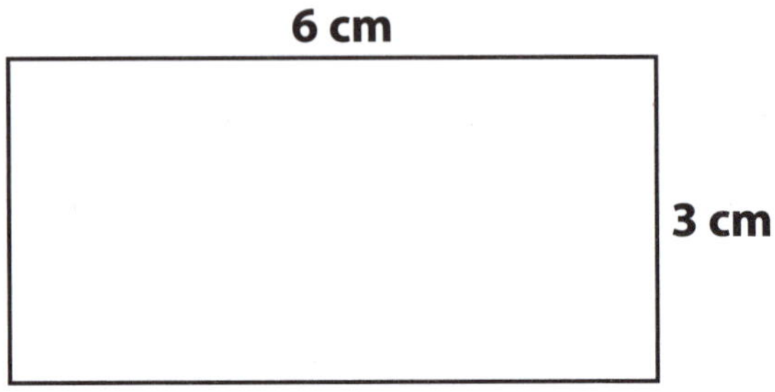

Perimeter = _____ cm

c Perimeter = _____ cm

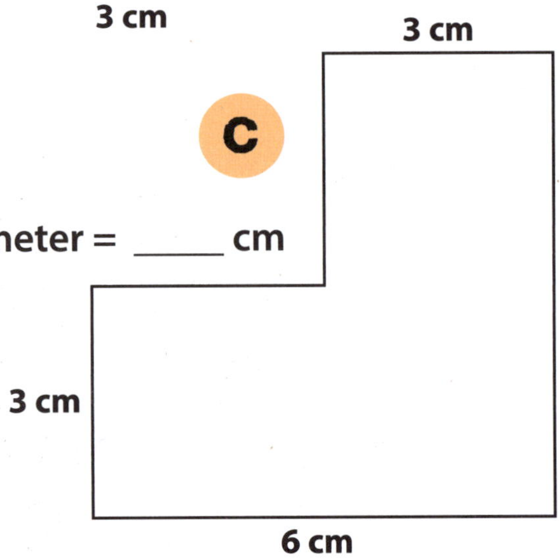

d

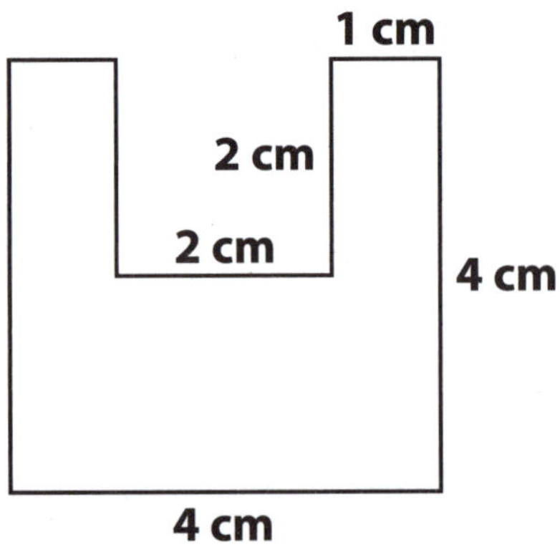

Perimeter = _____ cm

Measure these shapes and find the perimeter.

a

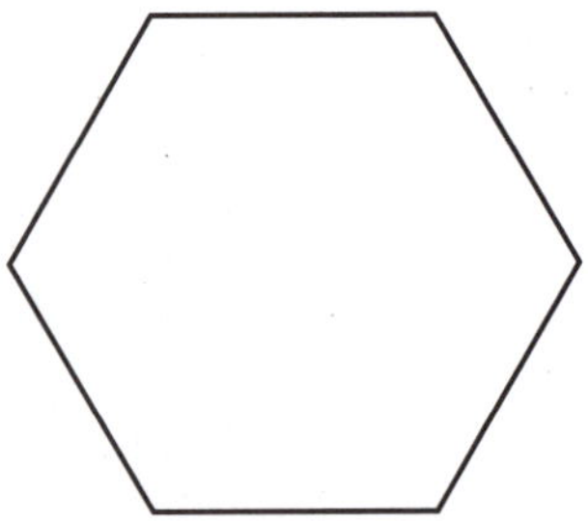

Perimeter = _____ cm

b

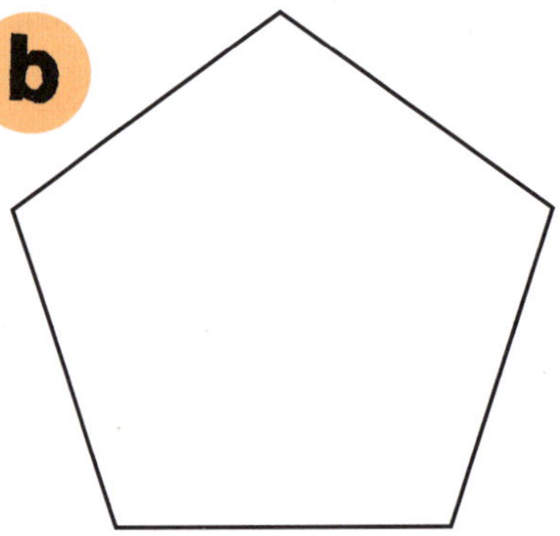

Perimeter = _____ cm

c

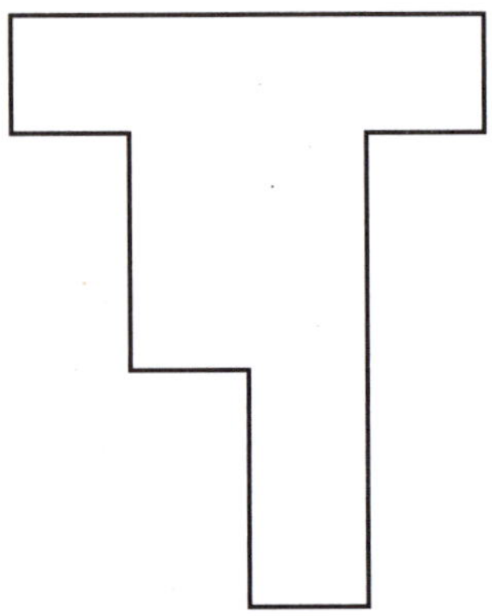

Perimeter = _____ cm

The **area** is the measurement of the space inside the shape.

To find the area of a shape you multiply the length by the width.

For example:

This rectangle has an area of 8 cm^2.

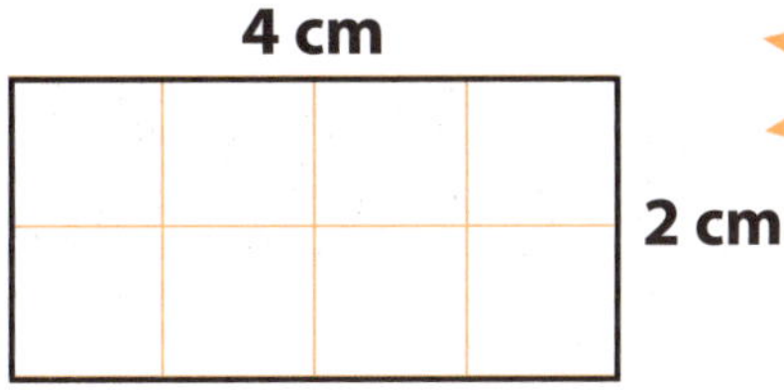

get it?

Area = length x width

So, 4 x 2 = 8 cm^2.

Find the area of these shapes.

You might have to divide complex shapes into rectangles to work out the area.

These shapes are not to scale.

a

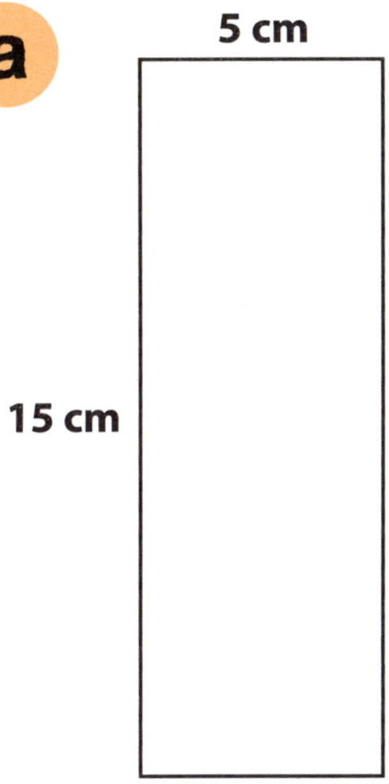

b

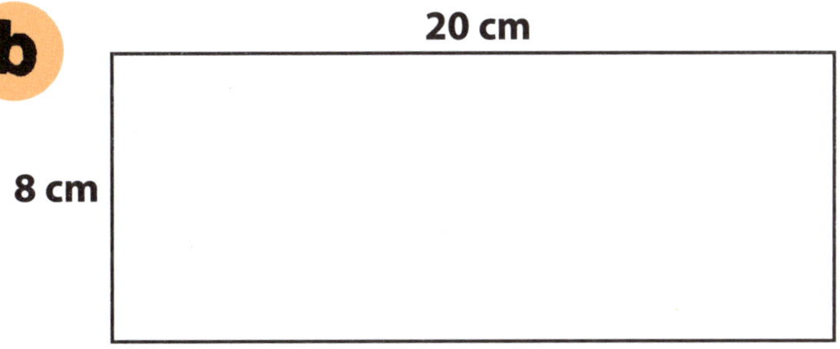

c

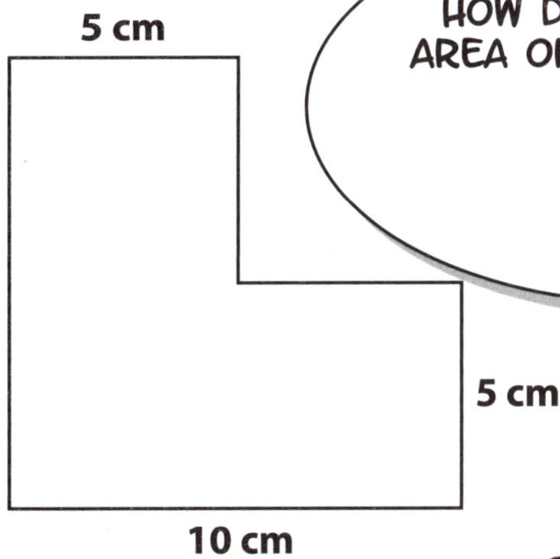

d

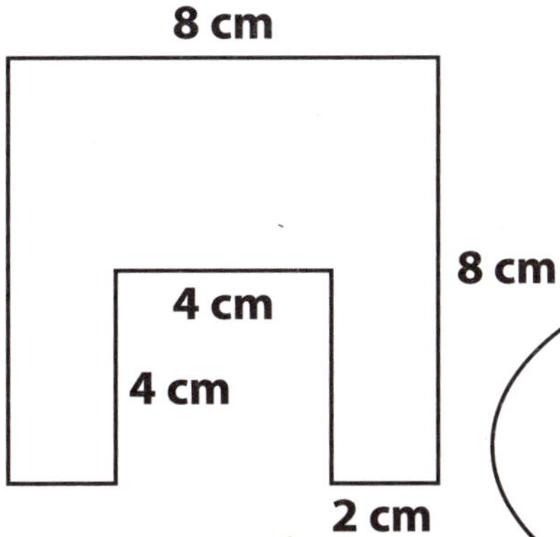

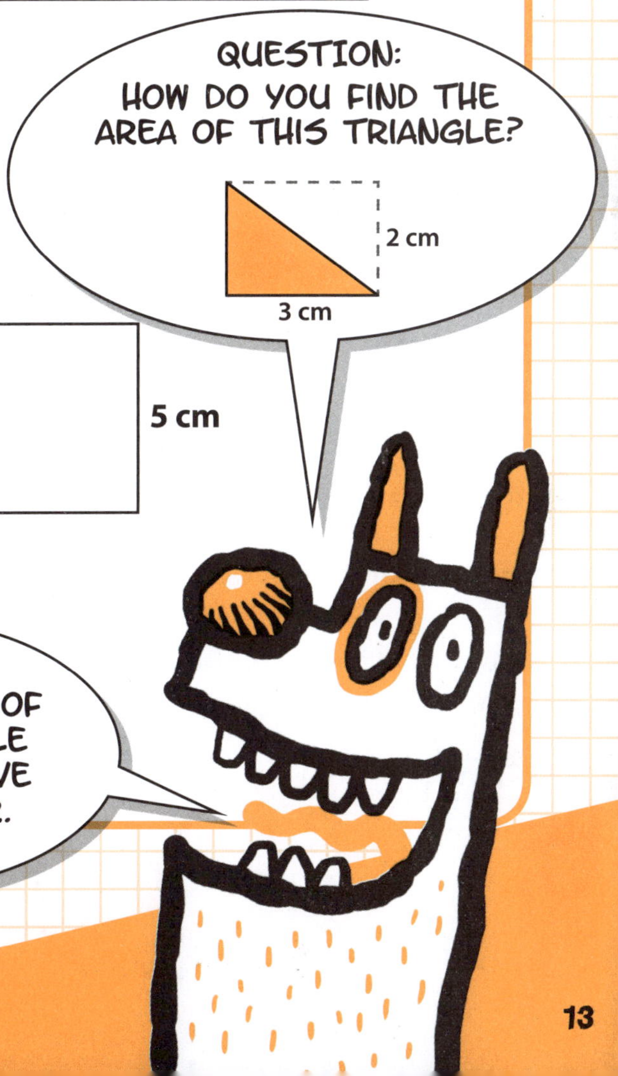

fractions and percentages

stick a reward sticker here!

$\frac{1}{4}$ means 1 part out of 4 equal parts.

$\frac{3}{4}$ means 3 parts out of 4 equal parts.

What fraction of these shapes is shaded?

a

b

c

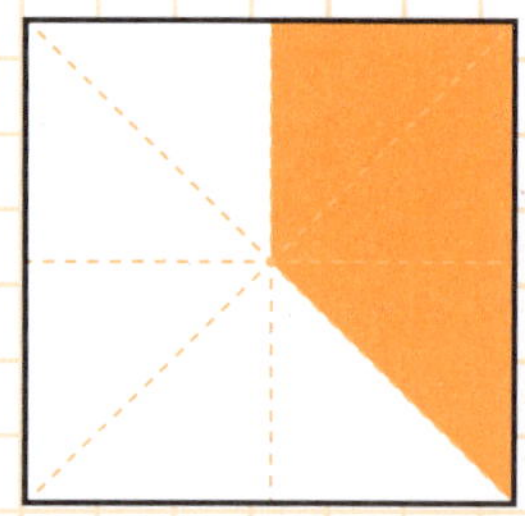

You can **simplify** fractions if you can divide the top number and the bottom number by the same factor.

For example:

$\frac{2}{6} = \frac{1}{3}$

Divide the numerator $2 \div 2 = 1$

Divide the denominator $6 \div 2 = 3$

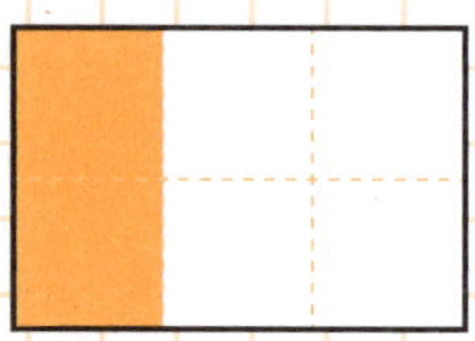

Simplify these fractions:

a. $\frac{4}{10} = \text{—}$ **b.** $\frac{3}{6} = \text{—}$ **c.** $\frac{8}{16} = \text{—}$ **d.** $\frac{4}{16} = \text{—}$

e. $\frac{5}{10} = \text{—}$ **f.** $\frac{2}{10} = \text{—}$ **g.** $\frac{3}{12} = \text{—}$ **h.** $\frac{4}{12} = \text{—}$

get it?

$\frac{6}{6}$ **is one whole.** $\frac{10}{10}$ **is one whole.** $\frac{12}{12}$ **is one whole.**

A **percentage** is a part of a hundred.

Learn these fraction and percentage equivalents.

10% or $\frac{1}{10}$									
20% or $\frac{1}{5}$				
25% or $\frac{1}{4}$			
50% or $\frac{1}{2}$	
100% or 1 whole

Work out the answers.

a. $\frac{1}{2}$ of 50 = ___

b. 50% of 30 = ___

c. $\frac{1}{4}$ of 4 = ___

d. 25% of 8 = ___

e. $\frac{1}{5}$ of £2.50 = ___p

f. 20% of £5 = £___

g. $\frac{2}{5}$ of 25p = ___p

h. 40% of 30p = ___p

i. 10% of £4 = ___p

j. $\frac{1}{10}$ of £8 = ___p

get it?

1% is 1/100

10% is 10/100

20% is 20/100

fractions

stick a reward sticker here!

Colour $\frac{1}{4}$ of this circle red.

Colour $\frac{1}{2}$ of this circle blue.

What is the total fraction coloured?

Which is bigger?

A slice that is $\frac{2}{3}$ or $\frac{3}{4}$ of this pizza?

Colour the pizza to work it out.

Which is bigger?

a. $\frac{5}{8}$ or $\frac{1}{4}$? ______

b. $\frac{3}{8}$ or $\frac{3}{4}$? ______

c. $\frac{4}{12}$ or $\frac{4}{6}$? ______

d. $\frac{5}{12}$ or $\frac{2}{3}$? ______

e. $\frac{4}{6}$ or $\frac{1}{3}$? ______

get it?

A **fraction** is an equal part of a whole.

get it?

$\frac{5}{10}$ and $\frac{1}{2}$ are **equivalent** fractions!

Write these fractions in the correct place on the number line below.

0 — 1

$\frac{1}{2}$ $\frac{1}{5}$ $\frac{10}{10}$ $\frac{1}{10}$ $\frac{7}{10}$ $\frac{2}{5}$ $\frac{3}{10}$ $\frac{4}{5}$ $\frac{5}{10}$

Which two fractions have the same value?

Join the equivalent fractions with a line.

$\frac{2}{3}$ $\frac{2}{4}$ $\frac{3}{12}$ $\frac{3}{9}$

$\frac{4}{6}$ $\frac{1}{4}$ $\frac{1}{3}$ $\frac{1}{2}$

Order these fractions from the smallest to the biggest.

$\frac{1}{2}$ $\frac{1}{4}$ $\frac{3}{4}$ $\frac{4}{10}$

smallest fraction — biggest fraction

angles and triangles

An **angle** is a rotation around a point.
We can measure an angle using a protractor.

There are four types of angles.

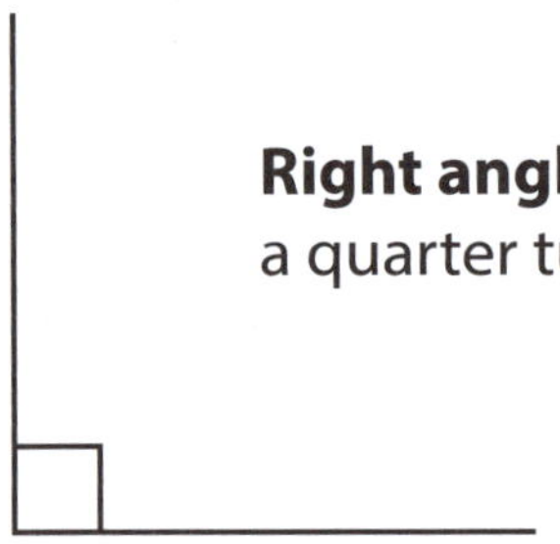

Right angle:
a quarter turn (90°)

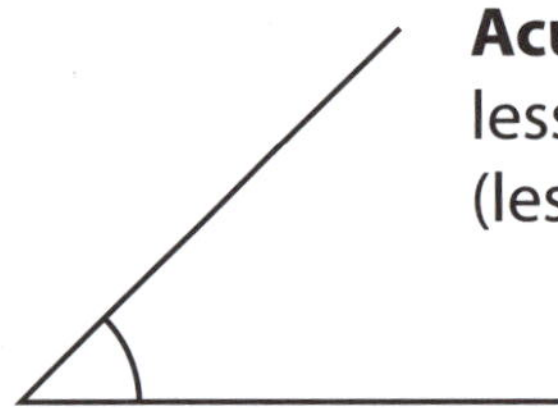

Acute angle:
less than a quarter turn
(less than 90°)

Obtuse: between a quarter and a half turn (more than 90° but less than 180°)

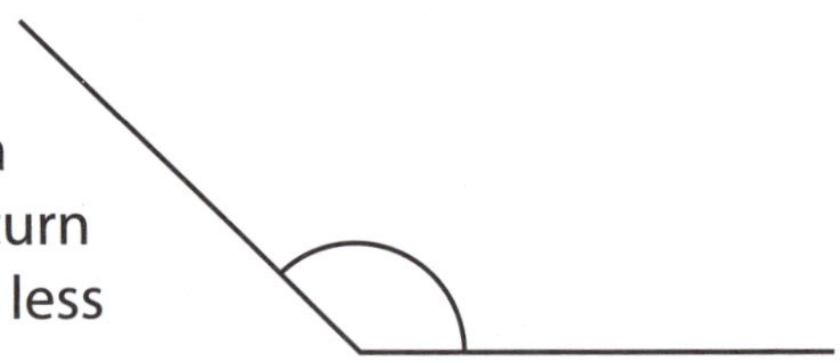

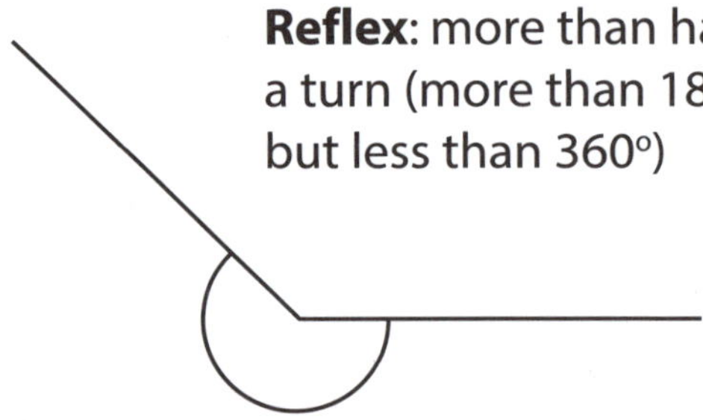

Reflex: more than half a turn (more than 180° but less than 360°)

* A complete rotation around a point is 360°.

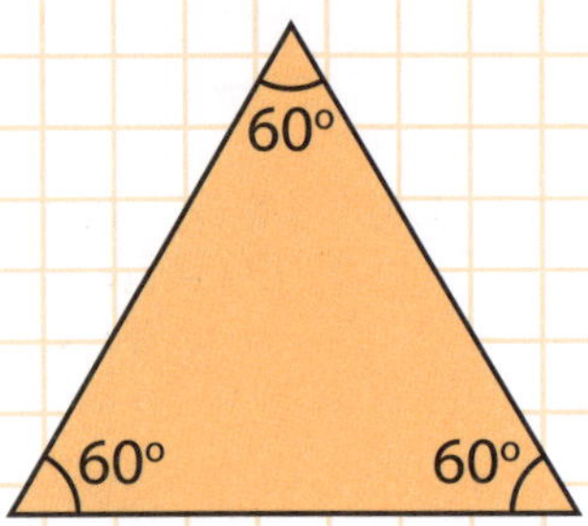

Equilateral: 3 equal sides and 3 equal angles

Isosceles: 2 equal sides and 2 equal angles

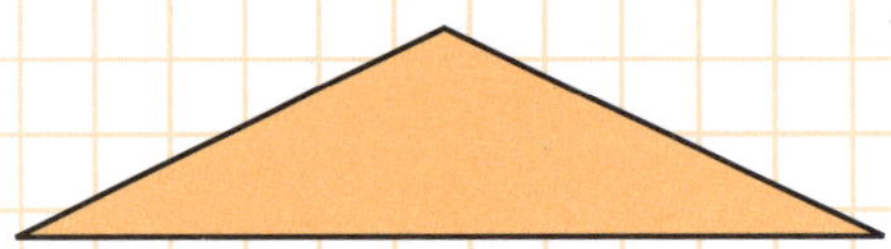

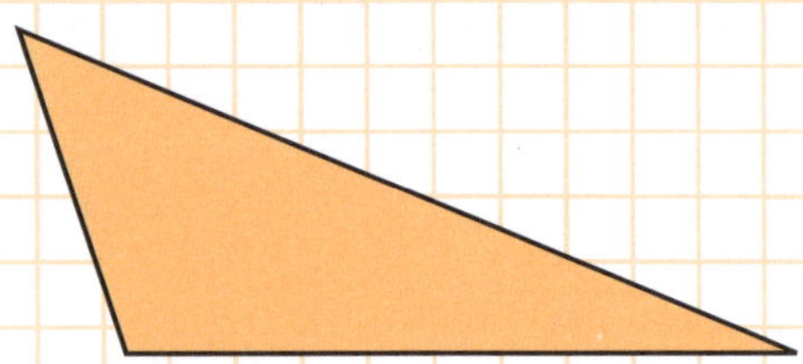

Scalene: no equal sides and no equal angles.

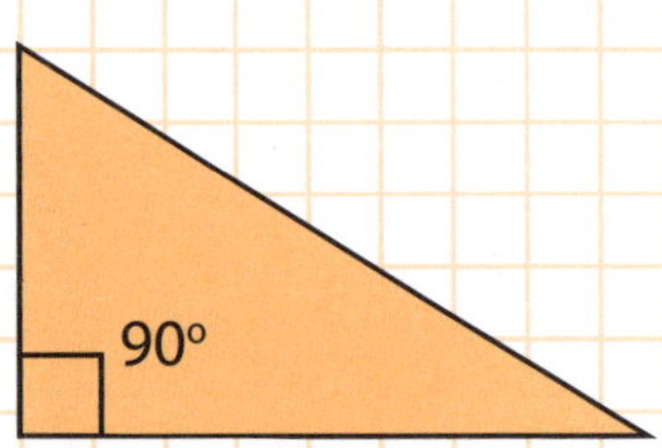

Right-angled:
one right angle

If you add up the angles in a triangle you always get 180°.

get it?

If you are given two angles, say 70° and 80°, you add these together and subtract them from 180 to find the missing angle.
180-150 = 30°.

Work out the missing angles in these triangles.

a.

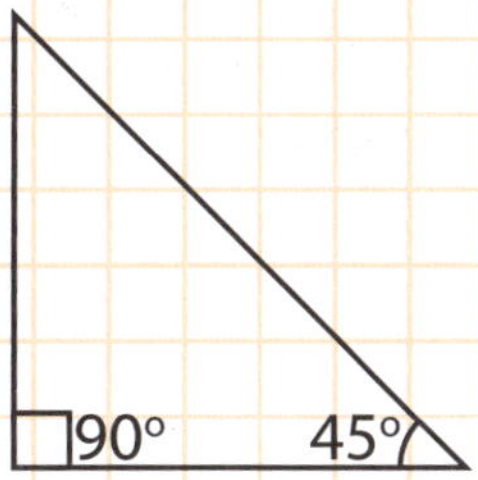

b.

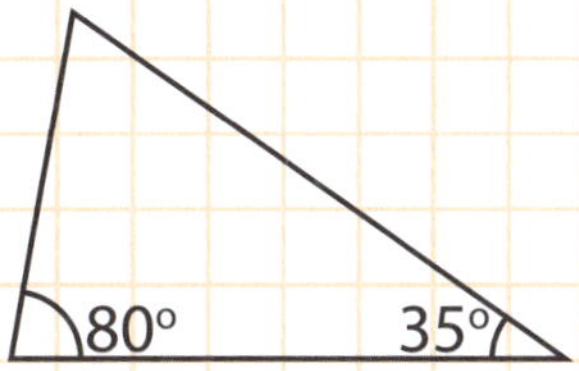

c.

d.

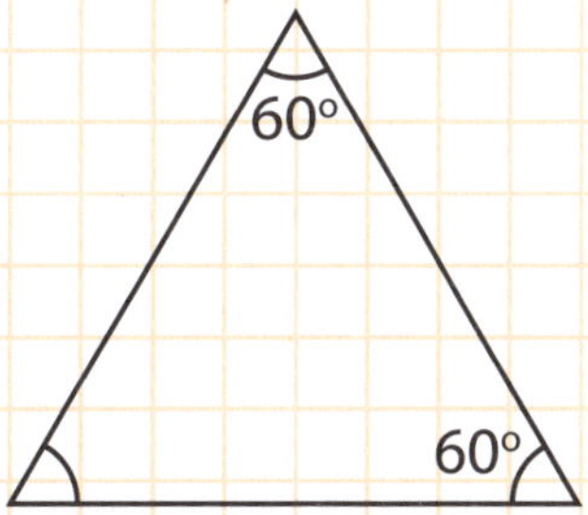

Label these angles: acute, right angle, obtuse or reflex.

a.

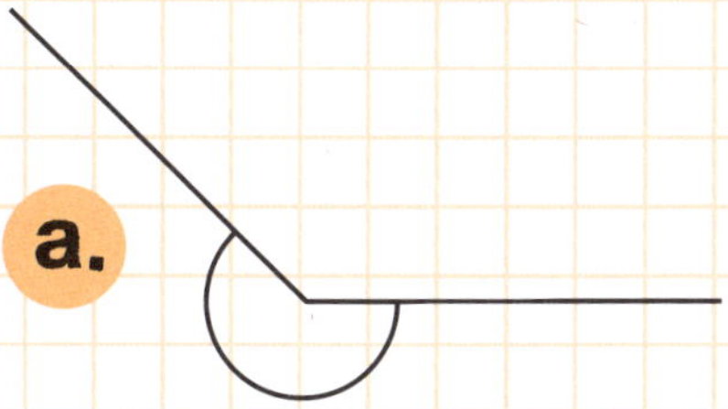

b.

c.

d.

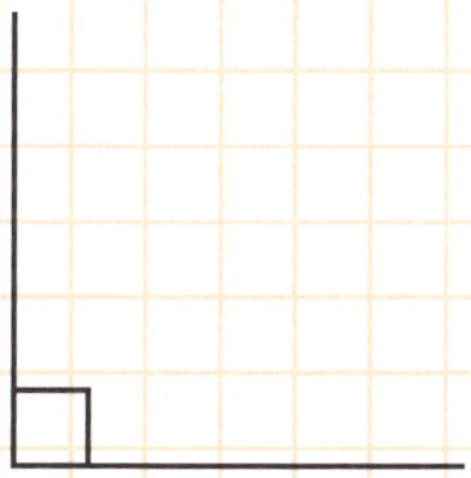

**Find the missing angles below.
Remember, they should add up to 360°.**

a.

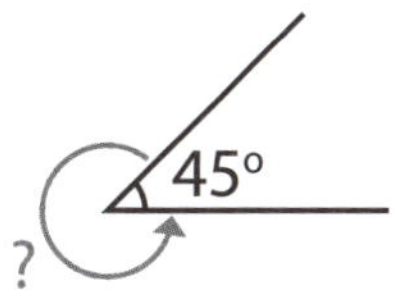

b.

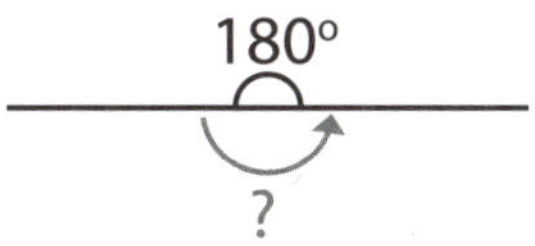

c.

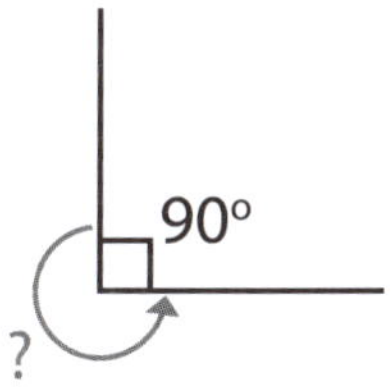

d.

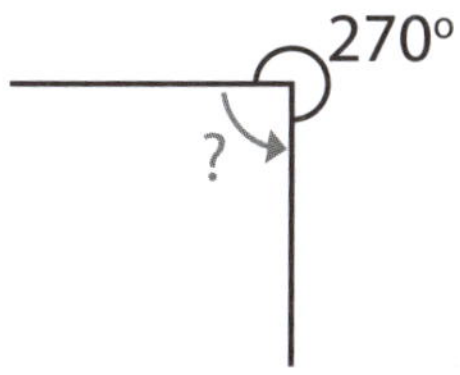

coordinates

Coordinates are the numbers we use to mark a point on a graph or map.

When reading coordinates, remember to '*go along the corridor and up (or down) the stairs*'.

get it?

Another way to remember how to read coordinates: x comes before y in the alphabet, so read the x axis first then the y axis.

Plot these positions on the graph.

a. (-2, 2) **b.** (-4, 4) **c.** (2, 2) **d.** (4, 4)

e. (-2, -2) **f.** (-4, -4) **g.** (2, -2) **h.** (4, -4)

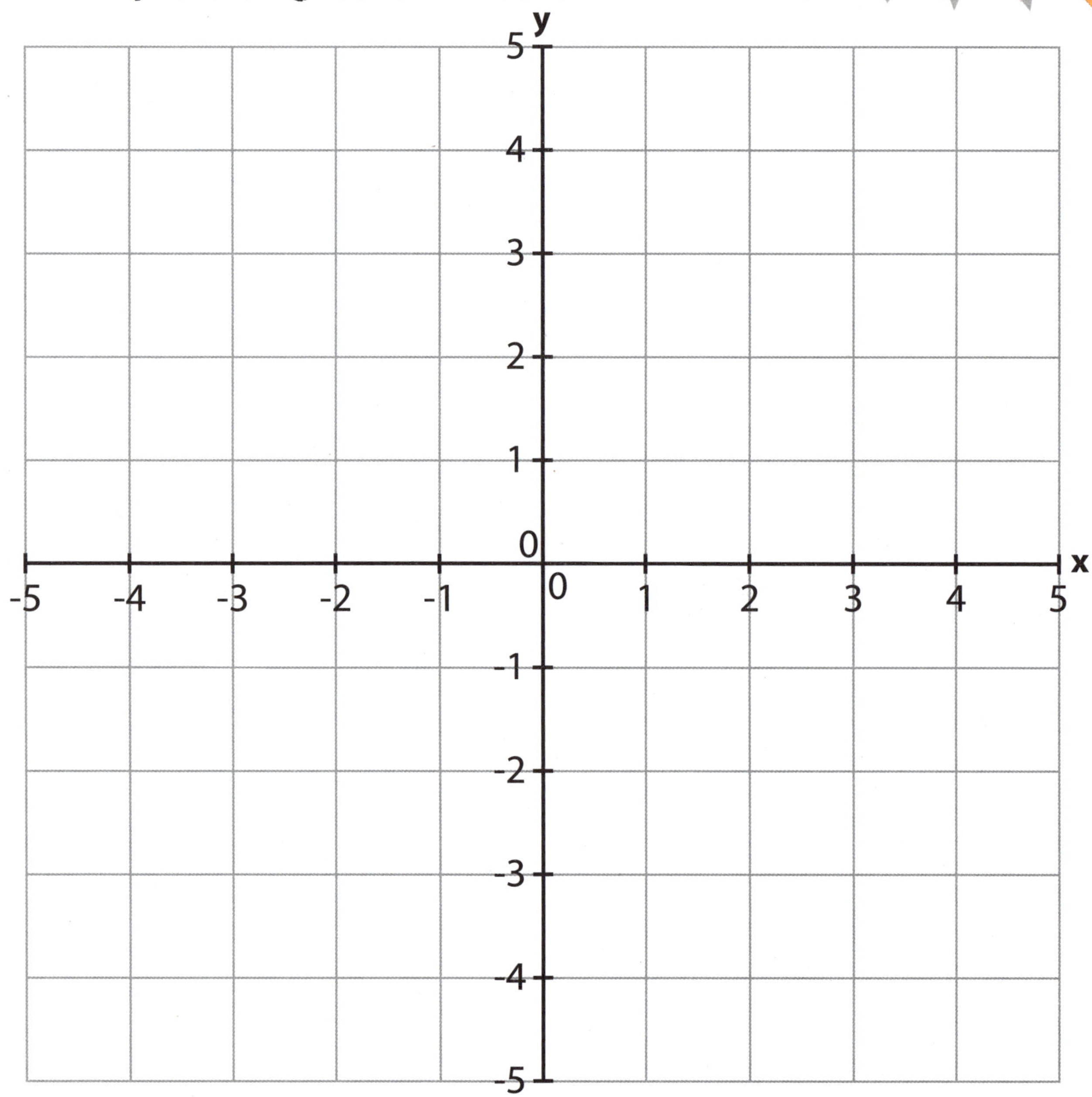

stick a reward sticker here!

Write the coordinates of the buried bone: (_____ , _____)

Draw another bone on the map and write its coordinates here: (_____ , _____)

Plot these coordinates to find a hidden shape.

(-4, -4) (-4, 2) (-2, 4) (-2, -2)

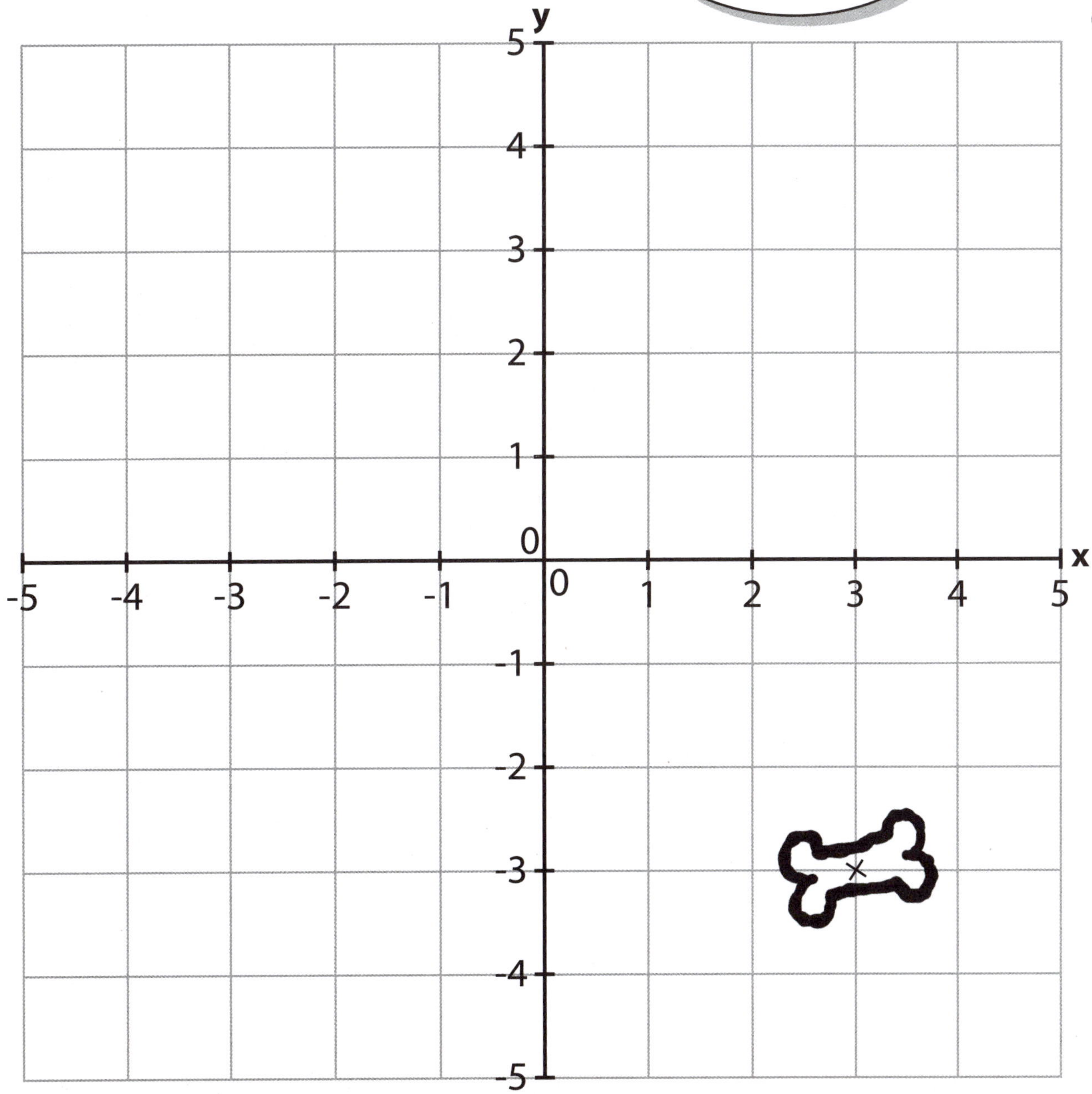

long multiplication

Here are two methods of doing long multiplication.

For example:

	H	**T**	**U**	
	2	4	2	
x		1	3	
2	4	2	0	*(x10)*
	7	2	6	*(x3)*
3	1	4	6	

Grid method:

X	**200**	**40**	**2**	**Total**
10	2000	400	20	= 2420
3	600	120	6	= 726

=3146

Find the answer to this multiplication using both methods.

	H	**T**	**U**	
	3	1	8	
x		2	5	
				(x20)
				(x5)

X	**300**	**10**	**8**	**Total**
20				=
5				=

=

Find the answers to these multiplications using both methods.

	H	T	U	
	3	2	6	
x		1	2	
				(x10)
				(x2)

X	300	20	6	Total
10				=
2				=

=

	H	T	U	
	4	0	4	
x		1	6	
				(x10)
				(x6)

X	400	0	4	Total
10				=
6				=

=

	H	T	U	
	2	1	3	
x		2	4	
				(x20)
				(x4)

X	200	10	3	Total
20				=
4				=

=

stick a reward sticker here!

long division

When you divide one number by another number, e.g. 28 divided by 7, it is like finding out how many 7s there are in 28. The answer is 4 because 4 x 7 = 28.

Look at this example:

7 | 2 8 7

We know that 28 ÷ 7 = 4 so 280 ÷ 7 = 40

Then 7 ÷ 7 = 1

The answer = 41

We can write it down like this:

```
    4 1
7 | 2 8 7
  - 2 8 0
        7
```

Now look at this example:

```
      5 0 r2
15 | 7 5 2
   - 7 5 0
         2
```

r = remainder

get it?

75 ÷ 15 = 5 so 750 ÷ 15 = 50.

Try these divisions for practice.

a. 20 | 4 8 0

b. 22 | 6 6 7

c. 14 | 5 7 4

d. 50 | 2 6 0

Always try to estimate your answers first.

For example:

Share £2.04 between 4 children.

You know that £2 ÷ 4 = 50p so you can estimate that £2.04 ÷ 4 will be a little bit more than 50p.

Now do the division to find out the answer ...

```
       5  1
  4 |2  0  4
  -  2  0  0
           4
```

Answer: £2.04 ÷ 4 = 51p

Work out these division problems.

Estimate your answers first.

1. Share £5.25 by 5 children.
2. Divide 568 by 8.
3. 901 ÷ 4
4. If Alice can run 5 kilometres per day, how long would it take her to run 125 kilometres?
5. If Dig eats 156 bones per year, how many bones does he eat per week?
6. If Kit sleeps 147 hours per week, how many hours does she sleep per day?

Do your working out here...

Now try dividing some longer numbers! Practise in the space below.

For example:

```
       2  4  1
12 |2  8  9  2    28 divided by 12 = 2 r 4
 -  2  4
       4  9       49 divided by 12 = 4 r 1
 -     4  8       12 divided by 12 = 1
          1  2
```

stick a reward sticker here!

decimals

A **decimal** is part of a whole number. It is similar to a fraction.

The number before the decimal point is a whole number. The number after the decimal point is a part of a whole number.

Read the decimals on the number line below.

These are tenths of a whole number.

0 — 1 — 2

0.0 0.1 0.2 0.3 0.4 0.5 0.6 0.7 0.8 0.9 1.0 1.1 1.2 1.3 1.4 1.5 1.6 1.7 1.8 1.9 2.0

Circle the decimal that is bigger in each pair.

a. 0.2 or 2.0

b. 1.2 or 2.1

c. 2.4 or 2.9

d. 3.6 or 0.6

get it?

$0.1 = \frac{1}{10}$

$0.2 = \frac{2}{10}$ (or $\frac{1}{5}$)

$0.3 = \frac{3}{10}$

$0.4 = \frac{4}{10}$ (or $\frac{2}{5}$)

$0.5 = \frac{5}{10}$ (or $\frac{1}{2}$)

Add or subtract these decimals just as you would do with any numbers.

Put the decimal point in your answer.

a
$$\begin{array}{r} 0.6 \\ +\,0.7 \\ \hline \\ \hline \end{array}$$

b
$$\begin{array}{r} 1.5 \\ +\,1.5 \\ \hline \\ \hline \end{array}$$

c
$$\begin{array}{r} 2.8 \\ -\,1.9 \\ \hline \\ \hline \end{array}$$

d
$$\begin{array}{r} 3.50 \\ -\,1.75 \\ \hline \\ \hline \end{array}$$

We use decimals in money.

For example:

1p can be written as 0.01

5p can be written as 0.05

10p can be written as 0.10

50p can be written as 0.50

£1.50 can be written as 1.50

Multiply and divide these decimals.

For example:

```
  £   2 . 5 0
  x         6
  -----------
  £ 1 2 . 0 0   (£2 x 6)
  £   3 . 0 0   (50p x 6)
  -----------
  £ 1 5 . 0 0
```

```
         3 . 2 0
   4 | £ 1 2 . 8 0
```

get it?

Try to estimate your answers first. Make sure you don't forget the decimal point – there is a big difference between £32.40 and £3240!

a. £2.25 x 4

b. £25.05 ÷ 5

c. £16.20 x 2

d. £28.21 ÷ 7

e. Share £14.40 by 6 children

f. 5 lots of 50p

stick a reward sticker here!

measures

Learn these equivalents:

1000 grams (g) = 1 kilogram (kg)

1000 millilitres (ml) = 1 litre (l)

1000 metres (m) = 1 kilometre (km)

1000 millimetres (mm) = 1 metre (m)

100 centimetres (cm) = 1 metre (m)

a. Kit can jump 2.5 m. How high is that in centimetres? ________ cm

b. Dig can run 5.4 km without stopping. How far is that in metres? ________ m

c. A quarter of a litre = ________ ml

d. 10 mm = ________ cm

e. Half a kilogram = ________ g

f. 1.50 kg = ________ g

g. 4.9 m = ________ cm

h. 3.2 litres = ________ millilitres

get it?

2.5 is the same as 2.50

5.4 is the same as 5.40

3.2 is the same as 3.20

a. Which is more: 1000 ml or 1 litre? ________

b. What is 25 kg as grams? ________ g

c. A fish tank holds 20 litres of water. How many millilitres is that? ________ ml

d. Dig weighs 10 kg. How much is that in grams? ________ g

e. Kit's bowl holds 250 ml of milk. How many bowls can be filled from 1 litre of milk? ________ bowls

f. Write 1200 g as kilograms. ________ kg

g. Convert 2.5 cm to millimetres. ________ mm

h. Which is longer: 300 mm or 3 cm? ________

stick a reward sticker here!

moving the decimal

stick a reward sticker here!

When we multiply a decimal number by 10 we move the decimal point **one** place to the **right**. When we multiply by 100 we move it **two** places. When we multiply by 1000 we move it **three** places.

For example:

4.9 x 10 = 49.00

4.9 x 100 = 490.00

4.9 x 1000 = 4900.00

We can leave out the zeros after the decimal point to simplify the number.

We do the opposite (we move the decimal point to the **left**) when we divide decimal numbers.

For example:

4.9 ÷ 10 = 0.49

4.9 ÷ 100 = 0.049

4.9 ÷ 1000 = 0.0049

Try these:

a. 1.35 x 10 = ________

b. 1.35 x 100 = ________

c. 1.35 x 1000 = ________

d. 1.35 ÷ 10 = ________

e. 1.35 ÷ 100 = ________

f. 1.35 ÷ 1000 = ________

get it?

If you run out of digits use zero as a place holder.

answers

p. 2-3 number values

a. fifty-three
b. six hundred and fifty-three
c. one thousand, six hundred and fifty-three
d. twenty-one thousand, six hundred and fifty-three
e. seven hundred and twenty-one thousand, six hundred and fifty-three

a. 2,304
b. 9,180
c. 11,376
d. 50,604
e. 201,890

a. 4201, 5345, 6032, 7436
b. 5386, 5642, 5740, 5900
c. 6001, 6201, 6389, 6945

a. 0.01, 0.59, 0.73, 0.90
b. 0.05, 0.09, 0.10, 0.21

negative numbers
-10 -9 -8 -7 -6 -5 -4 -3 -2 -1 0 1 2 3 4 5 6 7 8 9 10

a. -10, -7, -3, -1, 9, 10
b. -7, -2, -1, 4, 7, 9
c. -8, -4, -1, 0, 1, 5

p. 4-5 addition and subtraction

add
a. 908
b. 890
c. 3050
d. 3627
e. 7299
f. 6510

subtract
a. 289
b. 448
c. 563
d. 1094
e. 2502
f. 2829

p. 6-7 shapes

symmetry
The parallelogram has no lines of symmetry!

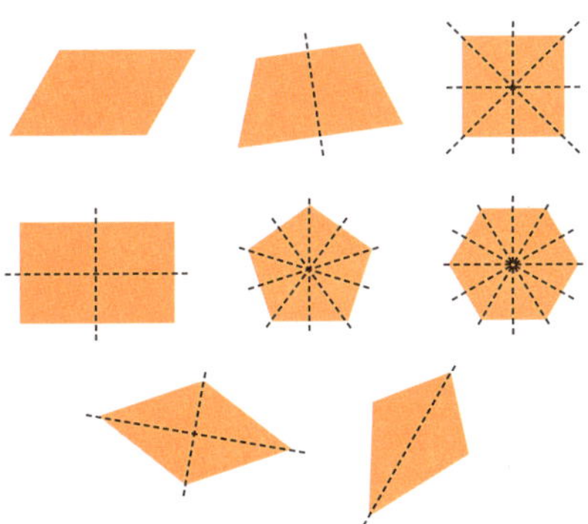

1. True
2. True
3. True
4. True
5. False

Shape	Number of faces	Number of edges	Number of corners (vertices)
Cube	6	12	8
Square-based pyramid	5	8	5
Triangular prism	5	9	6
Cylinder	3	2	0

p. 8-9 multiples and factors

count in 3s: 3, 6, 9, 12, 15, 18, 21, 24, 27, 30
count in 4s: 4, 8, 12, 16, 20, 24, 28, 32, 36, 40
count in 6s: 6, 12, 18, 24, 30, 36, 42, 48, 54, 60
count in 8s: 8, 16, 24, 32, 40, 48, 56, 64, 72, 80

multiples of 3: 36, 9, 30, 27, 21
multiples of 6: 36, 30
multiples of 4: 24, 40, 80, 28, 36
multiples of 8: 24, 40, 80

factors of 36
1 x 36
2 x 18
3 x 12
4 x 9
6 x 6

factors of 24
1 x 24
2 x 12
3 x 8
4 x 6

prime numbers: 11, 5, 13, 7

missing numbers
3 x 2 = 6
7 x 7 = 49
4 x 7 = 28
15 x 2 = 30
5 x 7 = 35

p. 10-11 division and multiplication

X	7	5	6	2
3	21	15	18	6
6	42	30	36	12
8	56	40	48	16
4	28	20	24	8

5 x 6 = 30
30 ÷ 6 = 5
30 ÷ 5 = 6

5 x 11 = 55
55 ÷ 11 = 5
55 ÷ 5 = 11

7 x 4 = 28
28 ÷ 4 = 7
28 ÷ 7 = 4

8 x 6 = 48
48 ÷ 6 = 8
48 ÷ 8 = 6

repeated subtraction
30 ÷ 5 = [6]
30 – 5 – 5 – 5 – 5 – 5 – 5

70 ÷ 10 = [7]
70 – 10 – 10 – 10 – 10 – 10 – 10 – 10

56 ÷ 7 = [8]
56 – 7 – 7 – 7 – 7 – 7 – 7 – 7 – 7

subtraction on a number line
15 ÷ 3 = [5] 15 → 12 → 9 → 6 → 3 → 0
20 ÷ 5 = [4] 20 → 15 → 10 → 5 → 0

p. 12-13 perimeter and area

a. 4 + 3 + 5 = 12 cm
b. 6 + 6 + 3 + 3 = 18 cm
c. 6 + 6 + 3 + 3 + 3 + 3 = 24 cm
d. 4 + 4 + 4 + 1 + 2 + 2 + 2 + 1 = 20 cm

a. 12 cm
b. 15 cm
c. 18 cm

area

a. 15 x 5 = 75 cm²
b. 20 x 8 = 160 cm²
c. 10 x 5 = 50 cm²
5 x 5 = 25 cm²
50 + 25 = 75 cm²
d. 8 x 4 = 32 cm²
2 x 4 = 8 cm²
2 x 4 = 8 cm²
32 + 8 + 8 = 48 cm²

area of the rectangle: 3 x 2 = 6 cm²
area of the triangle: 6 ÷ 2 = 3 cm²

p. 14-15 fractions and percentages

a. 8 out of 16 parts = 8⁄16 (or ½)
b. 4 out of 16 parts = 4⁄16 (or ¼)
c. 3 out of 8 parts = ⅜

a. 4⁄10 = ⅖ **b.** 3⁄6 = ½ **c.** 8⁄16 = ½
d. 4⁄16 = ¼ **e.** 5⁄10 = ½ **f.** 2⁄10 = ⅕
g. 3⁄12 = ¼ **h.** 4⁄12 = ⅓

a. ½ of 50 = 25 **b.** 50% of 30 = 15
c. ¼ of 4 = 1 **d.** 25% of 8 = 2
e. ⅕ of £2.50 = 50p **f.** 20% of £5 = £1
g. ⅖ of 25p = 10p **h.** 40% of 30p = 12p
i. 10% of £4 = 40p **j.** 1⁄10 of £8 = 80p

p. 16-17 fractions

9⁄12 (or ¾) is coloured
¾ (or 9⁄12) is bigger than ⅔ (or 8⁄12)

a. ⅝ is bigger than ¼
b. ¾ is bigger than ⅜
c. 4⁄6 is bigger than 4⁄12
d. ⅔ (or 8⁄12) is bigger than 5⁄12
e. 4⁄6 (or ⅔) is bigger than ⅓

number line fractions

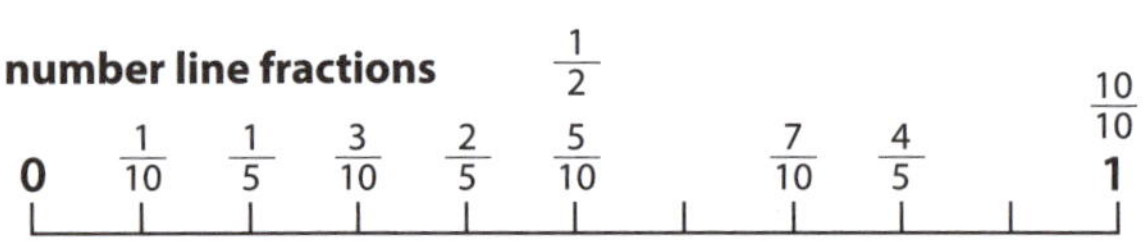

4⁄6 = ⅔
3⁄12 = ¼
3⁄9 = ⅓
2⁄4 = ½

smallest to biggest fraction: ¼, 4⁄10, ½, ¾

p. 18-19 angles and triangles

a. 45° **a.** reflex **a.** 45°, 315°
b. 80°, 35°, 65° **b.** acute **b.** 180°, 180°
c. 30°, 30°, 120° **c.** obtuse **c.** 90°, 270°
d. 60°, 60°, 60° **d.** right-angle **d.** 270°, 90°

p. 20-21 coordinates

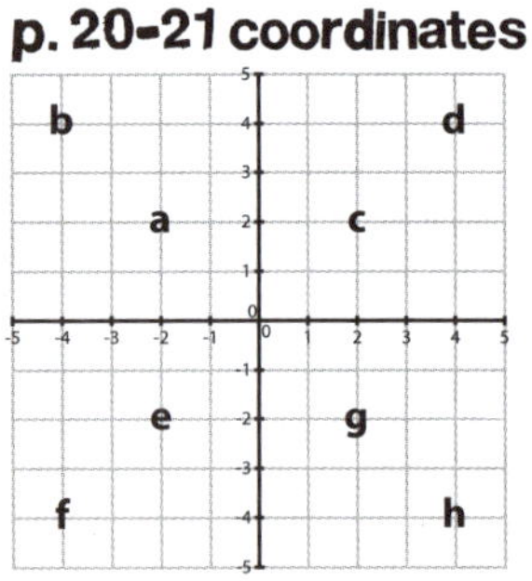

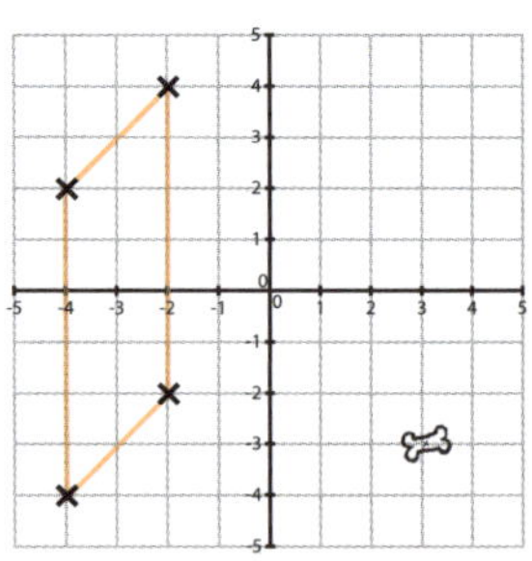

The coordinates for the bone are: [3, -3].
The coordinates [-4, -4] [-4, 2] [-2, 4] [-2, -2] form a parallelogram.

p. 22-23 long multiplication

```
  H T U
  3 1 8
x   2 5
6 3 6 0 (x20)
1 5 9 0 (x5)
7 9 5 0
```

X	300	10	8	Total
20	6000	200	160	= 6360
5	1500	50	40	=1590
				=7950

```
  H T U
  3 2 6
x   1 2
3 2 6 0 (x10)
  6 5 2 (x2)
3 9 1 2
```

X	300	20	6	Total
10	3000	200	60	= 3260
2	600	40	12	= 652
				=3912

```
  H T U
  4 0 4
x   1 6
4 0 4 0 (x10)
2 4 2 4 (x6)
6 4 6 4
```

X	400	0	4	Total
10	4000	0	40	= 4040
6	2400	0	24	=2424
				=6464

```
  H T U
  2 1 3
x   2 4
4 2 6 0 (x20)
  8 5 2 (x4)
5 1 1 2
```

X	200	10	3	Total
20	4000	200	60	= 4260
4	800	40	12	= 852
				=5112

p. 24-25 long division

a. 24
b. 30 r 7
c. 41
d. 5 r 10

1. £1.05 each
2. 71
3. 225 r 1
4. 25 days

5. 3 bones per week
6. 21 hours per day

p. 26-27 decimals

a. 2.0
b. 2.1
c. 2.9
d. 3.6

a. 1.3
b. 3.0
c. 0.9
d. 1.75

a. £2.25 x 4 = £9.00
b. £25.05 ÷ 5 = £5.01
c. £16.20 x 2 = £32.40
d. £28.21 ÷ 7 = £4.03
e. £14.40 ÷ 6 = £2.40
f. 5 x 50p = £2.50

p. 28-29 measures

a. 2.5 m = 250 cm
b. 5.4 km = 5400 m
c. 1000 ml ÷ 4 = 250 ml
d. 10 mm = 1 cm
e. 1000 g ÷ 2 = 500 g
f. 1.50 kg = 1500 g
g. 4.9 m = 490 cm
h. 3.2 litres = 3200 millilitres

a. 1000 ml and 1 litre are the same.
b. 25 kg = 25,000 g
c. 20 litres = 20,000 ml
d. 10 kg = 10,000 g
e. 1000 ml ÷ 250 ml = 4 (bowls)
f. 1200 g = 1.2 kg
g. 2.5 cm = 25 mm
h. 300 mm (or 30 cm) is longer than 3 cm

p. 30 moving the decimal

a. 1.35 x 10 = 13.5
b. 1.35 x 100 = 135
c. 1.35 x 1000 = 1350
d. 1.35 ÷ 10 = 0.135
e. 1.35 ÷ 100 = 0.0135
f. 1.35 ÷ 1000 = 0.00135